The God of the Comeback

The God of the Comeback

*

Discovering Personal Recovery in the Christian Life

Written by: Roderick L. Evans

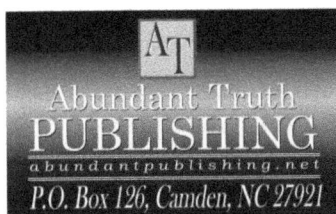

Abundant Truth
PUBLISHING
abundantpublishing.net
P.O. Box 126, Camden, NC 27921

The God of the Comeback

Discovering Personal Recovery in the Christian Life

Front & Back Cover Designs by Abundant Truth Publishing

Abundant Truth Publishing
an imprint of Abundant Truth International Ministries

For information address:
Abundant Truth International
P.O. Box 126
Camden, NC 27921

ISBN 13: 978-1-60141-295-9

Printed in the United States of America

Contents

Preface

Introduction

Preface

Overcoming failure is part of our life's journey. Failures seem bigger when they occur in one's relationship with the Lord. Therefore, feelings of guilt and shame plaque many members in the Body of Christ. However, there is hope in Jesus Christ.

This second book of this series is written to continue to encourage believers in their walks with the Lord. It is our prayer that through the information presented, believers will forget the failures of the past and press forward in their relationships with God.

Roderick L. Evans

Introduction

How do you handle personal mistakes? Do you allow them to paralyze your personal success and spiritual growth? Or, do you allow them to induce fear and doubt in your relationship with Christ? The Bible contains numerous accounts of individuals who failed in their relationship with Him. Yet, this did not prevent them from doing great things for Him.

God is a God of the Comeback. In the second book of this series, we will continue to examine the failures and ultimate successes of biblical characters. If they overcame, then, the Christian today can come out of any personal pit and enter into their God-given purpose. Their examples provide hope and strength for the Christian today. Book 2 of 2.

1

Who Hath Seen Such Things?

God is the source of the cosmos. All things exist by His will, volition, and awesome power. When a man enters into relationship with Him, he has the backing of all of heaven. God, in His great power, looks upon man and considers him. This inspired the Psalmist to ask,

> *What is man, that thou art mindful of him? and the son of man, that thou visitest him? Psalms 8:4 (KJV)*

In spite of man's ability to make bad decisions, God still visits and aids man in his daily existence. What a great comfort! Even in man's failure, God's faithfulness remains.

Many stand in doubt of God's willingness to restore and forgive, even after deliberate failure and disobedience. However, consider His words to Moses after Israel's rebellion in the wilderness,

> *For he saith to Moses, I will have mercy on whom I will have mercy, and I will have compassion on whom I will have compassion. Romans 9:15 (KJV)*

God chose to have mercy upon a people who repeatedly complained and rebelled.

Why? He had a plan for Israel as a nation. God delights in showing mercy. The ultimate expression of this was revealed in Christ coming to provide salvation to the world. Even when we have failed after coming to Him, He will have mercy that we can partake of His eternal plan of salvation.

In the first book of this series, "The God of Another Chance," we discussed Israel's rebellion in the wilderness. Yet, we saw God's faithfulness to the nation revealed ultimately in bringing their children in to the Promised Land. However, we discover that Israel continued to rebel after their entrance.

God sent the prophets to warn them. He allowed troubles to be upon them.

Their enemies defeated them. However, Israel would not return to God. They continued to worship other gods and participate in the abominations of the surrounding nations. Consequently, God evicted them from the land that He had given them.

Though the nation rebelled, God gave them a promise of restoration and reconciliation. The writings of the prophets verify God's plan for the nation's success, even after centuries of disobedience and rebellion. The book of Isaiah records,

Who hath heard such a thing? who hath seen such things? Shall the earth be made to bring forth in one day? or shall a nation be

born at once? for as soon as Zion travailed, she brought forth her children. Shall I bring to the birth, and not cause to bring forth? saith the LORD: shall I cause to bring forth, and shut the womb? saith thy God. Isaiah 66:8-9 (KJV)

Israel, as a nation, would be diminished and scattered, but God promised two major features to their recovery – *restoration* and *reconciliation*.

The God of Restoration

God promised the nation that it would be fruitful and bring forth. Though many lives were lost and it seemed like they would be extinct, God would restore.

5

God specializes in restoring the lives of people. Israel's history reflects this throughout the pages of the Bible. Since He will not change, the Christian can be assured of His willingness to restore them in spite of negative events.

restore: to put or bring back into existence or use; to bring back to, or put back into a former or original stat

Restoration is provided to those who have suffered loss and setback. God's work of restoration through Christ does not end after accepting Him. He continues to restore those that have called on Christ's name.

Even as He promised Israel restoration through Joel's prophecy, Christians can expect the same.

> *And I will restore to you the years that the locust hath eaten, the cankerworm, and the caterpiller, and the palmerworm, my great army which I sent among you. Joel 2:25 (KJV)*

Israel experienced loss because of their actions, yet God promised to restore them. How much the more those who have believed on Christ? If a believer sins and offers sincere confession unto the Lord, he can expect restoration. Restoration not only in His walk with God, but also in natural things according to His will.

Many feel that if God forgives them, they

cannot expect anything else. They feel He will not give them another job if they messed a previous job up. Or, some feel they may never be able to operate in ministry because of failure. Others have similar feelings concerning other areas in their lives.

They have the mindset that "I knew better" or "it was my fault." Israel was at fault and God restored the nation. The Christian has to let God decide how He will restore and not "think" for God. The believer must submit to God, knowing He will forgive and restore.

Wherefore he saith, God resisteth the proud, but giveth grace unto the humble. Submit yourselves therefore to God. Resist the devil, and he will flee from you. James 4:6-7 (KJV)

Some think they are humble when they acknowledge their sins. True humility is reflected when you can admit your sin **and** receive God's forgiveness.

Some admit sin, but believe their feelings over what God has said. John told us that He is faithful and just to forgive us (I John 1:9). He will restore you as you trust in His faithfulness and abide in His love.

There is no fear in love; but perfect love casteth out fear:

because fear hath torment. 1 John 4:18 (KJV)

When we abide in His love, we strip the "pits" of guilt, shame, depression, and fear of their control. We are free to move forward and operate in the purposes of God.

The God of Reconciliation

As we consider our opening verses from Isaiah chapter 66, God concludes His promise of restoration to Israel by declaring "saith thy God."

reconcile: to restore to friendship or harmony

God would restore the nation physically

and reconcile the nation to Himself spiritually.

> *Shall I bring to the birth, and not cause to bring forth? saith the LORD: shall I cause to bring forth, and shut the womb? saith thy God. Isaiah 66:9 (KJV)*

God reaffirmed His relationship with the nation. Some believers feel that their relationship with Christ will not be intimate and genuine after failure. This is not true.

Just as God planned to restore and reconcile Israel fully, Christians can expect full reconciliation of their relationship with Christ after failure. God through Christ came to reconcile the world.

The ministry of reconciliation continues after receiving Christ. Remember, the father of the prodigal son did not make his son become a slave (Luke 15:11-32). He entreated him as a son with all rights and privileges. Even when we find ourselves out of God's purposes and wandering in pits of sin, failure, and depression; God awaits our return to restore, reconcile and renew our relationship with Him.

We must be willing to let go of how we feel, else we will remain in whatever "pits" we have fallen in. **When you stay in your personal pit of depression, guilt, shame, and despair, it is a form of spiritual pride.** You set yourself up to reject full reconciliation in your relationship with God.

You must humble yourself and know that God is bigger than how you feel in your heart.

For if our heart condemn us, God is greater than our heart, and knoweth all things. 1 John 3:20 (KJV)

Our hearts can condemn us. It is a fact. However, we must embrace the greatness of God over the gravity of our feelings. When we do so, we can receive more of His grace. **His grace then empowers us to receive reconciliation** when we fall or when we are thrown into the "pits' of life. In turn, we can accomplish God's purpose for our lives.

In the pages to follow, we will continue our examination of notable biblical characters, which failed and sinned before the Lord. Their stories of failure, redemption, and destiny should inspire hope and freedom in believers today.

2

Why Didst Thou Not Tell Me That She Was Thy Wife?

Three of the world's major religions assert their descent from Abraham the patriarch: Judaism, Christianity, and Islam. These religions claim natural and spiritual ancestry in Abraham. Abraham is known for his relationship with God. God chose Abraham to leave everything familiar to him.

Now the Lord had said unto

__Abram, Get thee out of thy country, and from thy kindred, and from thy father's house, unto a land that I will shew thee. (Genesis 12:1)__

Because of his obedience and subsequent service to God, Abraham is known as the **Father of Faith**.

Abraham's life inspires men today to follow God. He serves as an example of trust and hope in the midst of impossible situations. However, Abraham did not always demonstrate the faith that would characterize his life and legacy.

His story serves an example of hope for believers who struggle in their faith and walk with the Lord. After Abraham obeyed

God's voice, there was a famine. Because of this, he went down into Egypt.

> *And there was a famine in the land: and Abram went down into Egypt to sojourn there; for the famine was grievous in the land. (Genesis 12:10)*

Abraham & Pharaoh

Before Abraham (Abram) and Sarah (Sarai) entered into Egypt, Abraham asked his wife to be deceptive. He did not want her to reveal that she was his wife. He asked Sarah only to say that they were siblings (half brother and sister).

> *And it came to pass, when he was come near to enter into Egypt,*

that he said unto Sarai his wife,
Behold now, I know that thou art
a fair woman to look upon:
Therefore it shall come to pass,
when the Egyptians shall see
thee, that they shall say, This is
his wife: and they will kill me, but
they will save thee alive. Say, I
pray thee, thou art my sister: that
it may be well with me for thy
sake; and my soul shall live
because of thee. (Genesis 12:11-
13)

Abraham previously had a supernatural experience with God. God made promises to Abraham of how he would bless him and multiply him. Yet, when he got to Egypt, he became fearful. He did not fully trust in the Lord as he should. If God made promises to him, they could not come to pass if he were dead. Abraham did not consider this. His fear seemingly made him forgetful of the promises previously made by God.

> *And I will make of thee a great nation, and I will bless thee, and make thy name great; and thou shalt be a blessing: And I will bless them that bless thee, and curse him that curseth thee: and in thee shall all families of the earth be blessed. (Genesis 12:2-3)*

If he believed in God enough to follow his command to leave all, then, he should have been able to believe that God would keep him in the midst of adversity.

However, he did not. His lack of faith and fear led to deception.

It is inevitable that believers will face challenging situations. Like Abraham, some do not walk in faith during these times, but give in to their fears. *Consequently, some Christians have lied and been deceptive to avoid negative situations and consequences.* Some are deceptive to keep jobs, get hired, gain promotions, and the like. Like Abraham, they did not walk in faith. Even now, some are gripped by guilt and shame for these actions, but there is hope.

Upon entering Egypt, Sarah was taken into custody by Pharaoh who wanted to make her his wife. Abraham's deception put his own wife in a vulnerable

position. Abraham even received goods
from Pharaoh to validate his deception.
The story tells us that Pharaoh entreated
Abraham well through his goods.

*And he entreated Abram well
for her sake: and he had sheep,
and oxen, and he asses, and
menservants, and maidservants,
and she asses, and camels.
(Genesis 12:16)*

Abraham put his wife in an
adulterous situation and profited by
it. Yet, we read of no discipline from
the Lord. We discover that God does
not correct Abraham, but he plagues
Pharaoh.

And the Lord plagued Pharaoh

and his house with great plagues because of Sarai Abram's wife. And Pharaoh called Abram and said, What is this that thou hast done unto me? Why didst thou not tell me that she was thy wife? (Genesis 12:17-18)

God protected Sarah by plaguing Pharaoh's house. He suffered the consequences for Abraham's deception. Abraham did not suffer for his deception and left with the goods that Pharaoh had given him.

And Pharaoh commanded his men concerning him: and they sent him away, and his wife, and all that he had. (Genesis 12:20)

Some might argue that Abraham did not know God well enough to trust him. This occurred towards the beginning of his relationship with Him. This is why God was merciful to him.

It is true that God will be gracious to believers in times of weakness. ***However, our weaknesses and lack of experiences should not cause us to walk in doubt.*** Abraham and Sarah could have experienced some negative repercussions for their actions, but God was gracious.

Continuing our examination of Abraham, we discover that the Father of Faith demonstrated a lack of faith again. ***As believers, sometimes we commit the same sins and fail in the same areas***

repeatedly. He failed to believe that God had the power over life and death. He did not believe that God would spare his life in order to perform His promises to him. Abraham recovered and so will the believer.

Abraham & Abimelech

Though no excuse can be offered for Abraham's deception in Egypt, some may want to argue that it was his first faith challenge while following the Lord. Yet, Abraham committed the same offense after God established relationship and covenant with him.

Before coming into the land of Gerar, Abraham experienced God's presence in various ways. Abraham trusted God enough to protect him during the battle of the five kings. He and his men freed Lot and the kings of Sodom and Gomorrah.

After this, God revealed his promise of an heir to him. God calls him friend and reveals His plan to destroy Sodom. Abraham witnesses God's power when He executed His judgment on Sodom. Finally, God changes his and Sarah's name and establishes covenant.

All of these things happened from the time he left Egypt until he entered into the land of Gerar. If anyone should have been able to walk in faith, it should have been Abraham. However, he failed to trust God and operated in deception. Again, he doubted God's power over life and death.

He feared he would be killed. He walked in fear in spite of God's promise.

> *And Abraham journeyed from thence toward the south country, and dwelled between Kadesh and Shur, and sojourned in Gerar. And Abraham said of Sarah his wife, She is my sister: and Abimelech king of Gerar sent, and took Sarah. (Genesis 20:1-2)*

The same thing happened in Gerar as in Egypt. Abraham lied and Sarah was taken. Again, we discover that God does not correct Abraham, but threatens Abimelech in a dream.

> *But God came to Abimelech in a dream by night, and said to him,*

Behold, thou art but a dead man, for the woman which thou hast taken; for she is a man's wife. (Genesis 20:3)

Believers have to remember testimonies of God's deliverance and help in their lives. This will help them to believe God in times of trouble. It will help the believer to avoid sin and error.

God warns Abimelech and then speaks well of Abraham. He tells Abimelech that Abraham will pray for him and his house.

Now therefore restore the man his wife; for he is a prophet, and he shall pray for thee, and thou shalt live: and if thou restore her not, know thou that thou shalt surely

***die, thou, and all that are thine.
(Genesis 20:7)***

Though Abraham was a repeat offender, God was a repeat forgiver. God still spoke of Abraham's position before Him by calling him a prophet. In addition, God spoke of Abraham's relationship with him by telling Abimelech that he would pray for him.

There are believers today who believe they have ruined their lives and ministries because of sin and failure. ***This account reveals that if we continue in Him, God will not always remove us from our position (like Cain), and our relationship with Him will not be hindered.*** Abraham was still called a prophet and was expected to act as one.

Abraham prayed for Abimelech's house and God heard him. The women were able to conceive and bring forth children. God was still with Abraham and used him.

This is where some believers fail to believe God. *They feel that because they failed and others know their sins that they will not be able to minister effectively.* Moreover, some feel that God is incapable of using them. Abraham's story reveals the opposite.

After his deception, God used him with results. *If the believer continues to follow the Lord and forsake known sins, God will use him also.*

Abraham's failure in Egypt and Gerar

show that believers can fail repeatedly in the same areas. The key to overcoming is to continue to follow Christ until victory is achieved. These two accounts demonstrate that God was interested in blessing Abraham and not cursing him.

God was merciful to him for He knew the man that Abraham would become in Him. *God is merciful to us in times of sin and failure for He knows who we will become in Him also.*

Even after these two accounts of failure, Abraham's faith was perfected and he received the blessing of the Lord. In each of these stories, Abraham left with wealth and substance.

And Abimelech took sheep, and oxen, and menservants, and womenservants, and gave them unto Abraham, and restored him Sarah his wife. (Genesis 20:14)

This has spiritual implications for the believer. *Faults and failures can teach believers valuable lessons.* That is, God can use the error to impart a greater knowledge of His character. Believers may sin and fail, but if they continue to walk with Him, they will leave their place of failure with treasures of wisdom and knowledge.

Abraham and Isaac

God fulfilled His promise to Abraham. His old, barren wife brought forth the child, Isaac. Abraham experienced God's power in the midst of an impossible situation. Yet, God would challenge Abraham's faith again.

> *And the Lord visited Sarah as he had said, and the Lord did unto Sarah as he had spoken. For Sarah conceived, and bare Abraham a son in his old age, at the set time of which God had spoken to him. (Genesis 21:1-2)*

Abraham had failed to believe in God's power over life and death previously. He did not trust fully in God's power to protect him from death. This is the reason he and Sarah were deceptive in Egypt and in Gerar. God, however, allowed Abraham to redeem himself.

***God will allow believers to come
face to face with past failures. He does
not do it to embarrass them or set them
up for failure, but to show them who
they are in Him.*** God allows believers to
redeem themselves from known sins and
failures. If you have failed in certain areas,
you can be assured you will have to face
them again: not to fail, but to succeed.

Though God gave Abraham promises
concerning the child that would come from
him, God commanded him to sacrifice the
child.

> ***And he said, Take now thy son,
> thine only son Isaac, whom thou
> lovest, and get thee into the land
> of Moriah; and offer him there for
> a burnt offering upon one of the***

mountains which I will tell thee of. (Genesis 22:2)

In his area of failure was Abraham tested. If God made promises concerning Isaac, Abraham had to believe that God would raise him from the dead if he were killed. The New Testament reveals that he did,

By faith Abraham, when he was tried, offered up Isaac: and he that had received the promises offered up his only begotten son, Of whom it was said, That in Isaac shall thy seed be called: Accounting that God was able to raise him up, even from the dead; from whence also he received him in a figure. (Hebrews 11:17-19)

Abraham's area of failure became his area of strength. Previously, he did not believe fully in God's power to bring back from the dead. He feared for his own life. However, he overcame his doubts and fears and believed that if Isaac died, God would raise him up again. ***This demonstrates to believers that God will cause areas of sin and failure to become a powerful testimony.*** Because of his act of faith, God gave Abraham an oath and swore by Himself.

> ***And said, By myself have I sworn, saith the Lord, for because thou hast done this thing, and hast not withheld thy son, thine only son: That in blessing I will bless thee, and in multiplying I will multiply thy seed as the stars of the***

heaven, and as the sand which is upon the sea shore; and thy seed shall possess the gate of his enemies; And in thy seed shall all the nations of the earth be blessed; because thou hast obeyed my voice. (Genesis 22:16-18)

God was merciful to Abraham in his time of weakness. Because of this, he was able to grow and mature in his walk with the Lord. God, then, tested Abraham in the same area. God not only wanted to test Abraham, but bless him. He allowed Abraham to overcome his area of weakness and blessed him for it.

God does the same for believers. He is merciful to us in our failures. Then, He allows us to face them and overcome so that He can bless us. When Abraham passed this test, God pronounced the blessing upon him by saying, *"By myself have I sworn, saith the Lord, for because thou hast done this thing, and hast not withheld thy son, thine only son."* As we overcome sin and failure (through Christ's help), we will also receive the blessing of Abraham.

> *That the blessing of Abraham might come on the Gentiles through Jesus Christ; that we might receive the promise of the Spirit through faith. (Galatians 3:14)*

Abraham's story reveals that believers can overcome even after they have failed repeatedly. He failed to trust

God on two occasions. He jeopardized his life, Sarah's life, and their marriage. Nevertheless, God was faithful. ***Though sins and failures place believers in unnecessary circumstances, God is merciful while believers grow.*** If believers continue in Him, they will find themselves overcoming and becoming pillars of faith and righteousness in the Body of Christ.

3

What Is Thy Name?

The story of Jacob is one of the most challenging to interpret. From his birth to death, there are numerous contradictions of thought and ideology. Jacob's story reveals the depths of God's love and compassion. It shows God's ability to transform a lifetime of mistakes and faults into one of honor dignity, and respect.

It reveals that God's choice to love and bless an individual is irreversible. It demonstrates that no personal "pit" can stop God's purpose if we continue on in Him.

As it is written, Jacob have I loved, but Esau have I hated. (Romans 9:13)

Jacob's story is a true example of how God's favor is incomprehensible. God will bless, elevate, and forgive individuals in order to achieve His purpose in their lives. Believers can learn the depths of God's love for them through Jacob's life. Even after a lifetime of fault and failure, God can cause believers to be carriers of His love, nature, power, and blessings.

Jacob's Birth

Rebekah, Isaac's wife, was barren. Isaac prayed that she would conceive. In response to his prayer, Rebekah became pregnant.

And Isaac intreated the Lord for his wife, because she was barren: and the Lord was intreated of him, and Rebekah his wife conceived. (Genesis 25:21)

Rebekah began to have troubles during her pregnancy and asked for understanding. The Lord responds to her.

And the Lord said unto her, Two nations are in thy womb, and two manner of people shall be separated from thy bowels; and the one people shall be stronger than the other people; and the elder shall serve the younger. (Genesis 25:23)

It is discovered that Rebekah is carrying twins and they are struggling in the womb. God reveals that the elder of the two will serve the younger; that is, the younger will be greater. At the time of delivery, an unusual thing occurs,

And the first came out red, all over like an hairy garment; and they called his name Esau. And after that came his brother out, and his hand took hold on Esau's heel; and his name was called Jacob: and Isaac was threescore years old when she bare them. (Genesis 25:25-26)

The first child is born covered with red hair so he is called Esau. When the second child comes forward, he catches the heel of the first; thus, he is called Jacob.

The name *Jacob* has various meanings, all of which are negative. Among the meanings are heel-catcher, supplanter, and deceiver. Because of his act at birth, the child received a name that would mark his life.

Jacob's birth reflects believers who have sinned. ***Because of their sin, some have been marked. When people see them and speak of them, they are identified by their acts of sin or failure.*** Thus, some are afraid that they will never be able to recover from the stigma attached to their names. However, we shall discover that Jacob overcame and the believer can also.

Jacob's Betrayal

Jacob grew up as a man of the house, while Esau was an outdoorsmen and hunter.

> **And the boys grew: and Esau was a cunning hunter, a man of the field; and Jacob was a plain man, dwelling in tents. (Genesis 25:27)**

Since Esau was the firstborn, he was entitled to the firstborn's birthright and blessing. However, Jacob obtained Esau's birthright. Contrary to popular belief, Jacob did not deceive or trick Esau for it.

> **And Jacob said, Sell me this day**

thy birthright. And Esau said, Behold, I am at the point to die: and what profit shall this birthright do to me? And Jacob said, Swear to me this day; and he sware unto him: and he sold his birthright unto Jacob. (Genesis 25:31-33)

Esau sold his birthright to Jacob with no deception or trickery. However, when Jacob's story is recalled, some cite this as a sign of his treachery. This is not true. It was an outright transaction.

Some Christians today experience the same reproach as Jacob. *Regardless of their actions, some are viewed negatively because of past indiscretions.* Even when there is no offense, they are still counted guilty. Yet, Christians have to know that there will be a time for vindication as there was for Jacob.

After Jacob obtained Esau's birthright by oath, the time came for Esau to receive the firstborn's blessing from Isaac.

> *And it came to pass, that when Isaac was old, and his eyes were dim, so that he could not see, he called Esau his eldest son, and said unto him, My son: and he said unto him, Behold, here am I. And make me savoury meat, such as I love, and bring it to me, that I may eat; that my soul may bless thee before I die. (Genesis 27:1, 4)*

Isaac instructed Esau to prepare some meat for consumption. This was the prelude to Isaac bestowing the blessing upon him. Because Jacob was favored by his mother (who remembered the words of the Lord), she instructed Jacob to pose as Esau to receive the blessing.

Now therefore, my son, obey my voice according to that which I command thee. Go now to the flock, and fetch me from thence two good kids of the goats; and I will make them savoury meat for thy father, such as he loveth: And thou shalt bring it to thy father, that he may eat, and that he may bless thee before his

death. (Genesis 27:8-10)

Jacob's betrayal of Esau and Isaac for the blessing was not his idea. Rebekah formulated it. Even after her proposal, Jacob did not want to do it. He did not want to be cursed.

> *My father peradventure will feel me, and I shall seem to him as a deceiver; and I shall bring a curse upon me, and not a blessing. And his mother said unto him, Upon me be thy curse, my son: only obey my voice, and go fetch me them. (Genesis 27:12-13)*

Rebekah insisted that Jacob listen to her. She stated that whatever curse should come upon him, she would receive it. This explains why Jacob was not punished for his betrayal of Esau and Isaac. Rebekah said she would assume all responsibility. And rightly so, it was her idea.

God is merciful to believers because Christ acts as Rebekah did. Christ died for the sins of man. When one sins, the curse or penalty of sin is placed upon Christ. This is how believers can overcome after times of great failure. Jacob, subsequently, obeys his mother, betrays his brother, deceives his father, and receives the blessing.

And Isaac answered and said unto Esau, Behold, I have made him thy lord, and all his brethren have I given to him for servants; and with corn and wine have I sustained him: and what shall I do now unto thee, my son? (Genesis 27:37)

Esau was mad and he had murderous intent for his brother. Thus, his parents sent him away. Now Jacob was in a terrible position.

And Esau hated Jacob because of the blessing wherewith his father blessed him: and Esau said in his heart, The days of mourning for my father are at hand; then will I slay my brother Jacob. Now therefore, my son, obey my voice; and arise, flee thou to Laban my brother to Haran. (Genesis 27:41, 43)

His deception put his life in danger. He had to leave his home. **Believers have to understand that sin will put their spiritual lives in jeopardy.** Though God is gracious, believers must avoid putting their walk with God at risk. Jacob is instructed to go to his uncle's house in the land of Haran.

Jacob's Bethel

Jacob obeys his parents and leaves for Haran. On the first night of his journey, Jacob has to sleep outside. He used stones as pillows. While asleep, he has an astonishing dream.

> **And he dreamed, and behold a ladder set up on the earth, and the top of it reached to heaven:**

and behold the angels of God ascending and descending on it. (Genesis 28:12)

Jacob sees a ladder connecting heaven to earth with angels descending up and down on it. At the top of this ladder, he sees a vision of God, who does not come to judge Jacob for his deception but establish covenant with him.

And, behold, the Lord stood above it, and said, I am the Lord God of Abraham thy father, and the God of Isaac: the land whereon thou liest, to thee will I give it, and to thy seed; And, behold, I am with thee, and will keep thee in all places whither thou goest, and will bring thee again into this

land; for I will not leave thee, until I have done that which I have spoken to thee of. (Genesis 28:13, 15)

Jacob had just deceived his father and betrayed his brother. God appears to him to bless him and not curse him. Oh the depths of God's goodness!

Some believers today are in fear of God's discipline because of their sins and failures. God revealed His plan for Jacob and did not recall his sin. Even after failure, believers have to realize that God's plan for their lives does not change.

If the believer focuses on God's purpose for their lives, they will

inevitably recover after failure, as Jacob did. Jacob renames the place Bethel (***House of God***) instead of Luz. He renamed it because of his encounter with the Lord.

Jacob's Breakthrough

Jacob reaches the land of Haran and sees Laban's daughter Rachel, whom he fell in love with.

> ***And Jacob loved Rachel; and said, I will serve thee seven years for Rachel thy younger daughter. (Genesis 29:18)***

Jacob works seven years for Laban to receive her as his wife. However, Laban gives him Leah, his older daughter, first.

He, then, works another seven years to marry Rachel also.

While with Laban, the Lord increased him (with children, wealth, and substance) in spite of Laban's attempt to defraud him.

And the man increased exceedingly, and had much cattle, and maidservants, and menservants, and camels, and asses. (Genesis 30:43)

After these things, God instructs Jacob to return home.

And the Lord said unto Jacob, Return unto the land of thy fathers, and to thy kindred; and I will be with thee. (Genesis 31:3)

Jacob's return home posed a few problems; therefore, God promises that He would be with him. The last time Jacob was home, his brother threatened to kill him. He had not faced his past indiscretion and did not know what would befall him when he saw Esau again.

Some believers today are gripped by fear because of past sins and failures. *As God commanded Jacob to go home for resolution, so the Lord will cause believers to face their downfalls.* In spite of his fears, Jacob obeyed the Lord.

Then Jacob rose up, and set his sons and his wives upon camels; And he carried away all his cattle, and all his goods which he had gotten, the cattle of his getting, which he had gotten in Padanaram, for to go to Isaac his father in the land of Canaan. (Genesis 31:17-18)

Jacob had to face his brother Esau. While returning home, God sent angles to meet Jacob. They were sent to Jacob as a sign of God's presence and protection.

And Jacob went on his way, and the angels of God met him. And when Jacob saw them, he said, This is God's host: and he called the name of that place Mahanaim. (Genesis 32:1-2)

The angelic host did not calm Jacob's fears. *Some walk in fear and regret because of their faults. God reaffirms*

His love for believers daily through the Holy Spirit's presence and His blessings. However, some stand in doubt of God's willingness to protect them from the consequences of sins and faults. Jacob still feared what would happen when he faced Esau.

Jacob sent messengers to Esau to discover Esau's intentions toward him. He became faint when he discovered that Esau was coming to him with four hundred men. Jacob's fears were upon him. He sent goods ahead of him to extinguish Esau's anger. While he remained behind, he is found wrestling with a man.

And Jacob was left alone; and there wrestled a man with him

until the breaking of the day. (Genesis 32:24)

Jacob wrestled with the man (who was the angel of the Lord) because of his fear. He would not quit until he received a blessing from Him. ***Believers have to be persistent in their resolve to follow the Lord after error.***

Jacob knew he had to face Esau and he wanted assurance of God's protection and blessing.

In order to confront and overcome past sins, believers have to seek God and pray for his guidance and protection for victory. Because of his persistence, Jacob received a blessing; signified by the changing of his name.

And he said unto him, What is thy name? And he said, Jacob. And he said, Thy name shall be called no more Jacob, but Israel: for as a prince hast thou power with God and with men, and hast prevailed. And Jacob asked him, and said, Tell me, I pray thee, thy name. And he said, Wherefore is it that thou dost ask after my name? And he blessed him there. (Genesis 32:27-29)

God blessed Jacob and changed his name to Israel. His identity changed from a heel-catcher, supplanter, and deceiver. Now, he is identified as a prince who had power with God and man. God does the same for those who have failed. *If one wrestles with Him as Jacob,*

God will bless them to overcome areas of weakness and fault. In addition, the sin and failure will no longer characterize their walk and identity.

God will restore respect even in the eyes of men. Jacob's first breakthrough was with his identity. God changed Jacob's perception of himself through his new name.

Believers who want to overcome faults and failures have to exchange self-perception for God's perception of them. Jacob had to change his name and call himself Israel. The believer has to change his/her self-perception and call him/herself forgiven, blessed, and the righteousness of God. This breakthrough in self-perception leads to the second breakthrough.

After these events, Jacob (Israel) meets Esau. To Jacob's amazement, Esau was no longer angry with him. Rather, he was overjoyed and wept when he saw him. Jacob had a breakthrough in his area of fault.

And Esau ran to meet him, and embraced him, and fell on his neck, and kissed him: and they wept. (Genesis 33:4)

God did not allow Jacob's past sin to destroy him. God facilitated reconciliation between Jacob's past and present at this reunion. Jacob did not have to explain anything to Esau or even make lengthy apologies. God did not allow the enmity between them to continue. Jacob was able to reconcile with Esau and return home in peace.

The second breakthrough of Jacob serves as an example of that which is prepared for the believer. God first wants the believer's perception of self to change. After this, God will facilitate the reconciliation between the believer's faults and future. God caused peace between Esau and Jacob.

God does the same for the believer. *He will not allow the sins and failures of the past to kill His plan and purpose for the believer's life.* Jacob experienced this and God does the same for believers today.

Believers who have failed and waiting for punishment and consequences should turn to the Lord as Jacob did. *They will find that God is gracious and does not delight in a believer's downfall.* He protected Jacob and blessed him. He changed his name and established covenant with him. *Because God does not change, believers today can stand in expectation* of the same provision of forgiveness, protection, and blessing.

4

Where Are Those, Thine Accusers?

The woman was caught in adultery. There was eyewitness proof that she was guilty as charged. The men that brought her to Jesus demanded justice. In fact, they had already judged her, but they wanted to proceed with punishment.

They presented her to Jesus, expecting Him to meet out discipline upon her according to the Law. However, Jesus disappointed the woman's accusers and surprised her in His response.

So, when they continued asking him, he lifted up himself, and said unto them, He that is without sin among you, let him first cast a stone at her. (John 8:7)

After these words, no man dared to stone the woman, realizing their own guilt before the Lord.

And they which heard it, being convicted by their own conscience, went out one by one, beginning at the eldest, even unto the last: and Jesus was left alone, and the woman standing in the midst. (John 8:9)

There are believers, today, in the same situation as the woman. **They have** *sinned, rebelled, complained, and failed God. Because of this, they continue to doubt God's favor upon their lives and they doubt that He will fulfill His promise to them.* In this final section, we will discuss what every believer can do to come out of the pit and enter into purpose.

The account of the woman taken in adultery provides the believer with the necessary tools for victory over past sins and failures.

Jesus' words to her can be applied to the life of the believer today.

When Jesus had lifted up himself, and saw none but the woman, he said unto her, Woman, where are those, thine accusers? Hath no man condemned thee? She said, No man, Lord. And Jesus said unto her, Neither do I condemn thee: go, and sin no more. (John 8:10-11)

Jesus' words give believers four steps to receiving God's promises in their lives after failure. Again, adherence to these steps will lead to one's personal 'Canaan.'

Walk in Freedom

There were men who witnessed this woman's sin. They, in turn, brought her to Jesus for judgment. After Jesus' response and the departure of her accusers, He asks the woman, "Where are those, thine accusers." In order for the woman to realize God's intent to spare her, she had to be freed from the influence of men. As long as her accusers were there, she would stand in doubt of God's forgiveness that was offered.

Some Christians are stunted because others know of their past sins and failures. *They do not receive God's forgiveness because men continue to accuse them and remind them of the error.* However, Christians who want to walk in God's promises have to free themselves from any guilt and condemnation at the hands of men. David expressed,

> *Against thee, thee only, have I sinned, and done this evil in thy sight: that thou mightest be*

justified when thou speakest, and be clear when thou Judgest. (Psalms 51:4)

David sinned greatly before the Lord. Though his sin affected people, he states that it was against God only. He committed adultery, lied, abused his power, and had an innocent man killed. In spite of these things, God spared him and fulfilled every promise made to him.

God does the same for believers. Yet, Christians have to realize, as David, that when they sin, it is against God. Though apologies may have to be expressed when sin affects certain individuals, the sin ultimately is only committed against God. David was able to recover, though he experienced some consequences, and become one of Israel's respected and notable kings. In addition, his life served as an example of the Christ who would come as king.

Walk in God's Forgiveness

Once the accusers departed, Jesus expressed that He did not condemn the woman for her actions. The next step for believers is to accept God's forgiveness. Some will not accept God's forgiveness because they have been repeat offenders. When teaching the disciples concerning forgiveness, Jesus taught that forgiveness should be given repeatedly. He was instructing the disciples to forgive like God.

But love ye your enemies, and do

do good, and lend, hoping for nothing again; and your reward shall be great, and ye shall be the children of the Highest: for he is kind unto the unthankful and to the evil. Be ye therefore merciful, as your Father also is merciful. (Luke 6:35-36)

Jesus stated that God is kind to the unthankful and evil; He is merciful. Even when we are ungrateful, unappreciative, and sinful, God remains merciful. This is because God does not delight in evil and destruction, but in blessing and restoration; which includes forgiveness.

The Lord is not slack concerning his promise, as some men count slackness; but is longsuffering to us-ward, not willing that any should perish but that all should come to repentance. (II Peter 3:9)

God does not want men to perish in their sins. This is why He sent Jesus. In addition, God does not want to revoke promises made to us. For this cause, He offers forgiveness to ensure we are in a position to receive from Him. The woman became a partaker of this truth.

Walk in Relationship

After Jesus grants the woman forgiveness, He simply tells her to go. She was to return to her daily living. He told her to go because she was forgiven. Before His words, she waited to see what He would say. Now, she was instructed to go on with life.

Believers who have sinned and failed sometimes find it difficult to recover and continue to walk in relationship with the Lord. Some, through prayer, stay at Jesus' feet waiting for some form of retribution or punishment.

Others feel they have to make up for what they did. Moreover, some feel they have lost their place in the Lord. But, Jesus told her to go; that is, carry on with life. There is life after sin and failure.

Jesus said unto him, Verily I say unto thee, That this night, before the cock crow, thou shalt deny me thrice. (Matthew 26:34)

Jesus warned Peter that he would deny Him. Peter rejected the warning and did so. He denied Jesus Christ three times in one night. Overcome with guilt and shame, Peter wept bitterly.

And Peter remembered the word of Jesus, which said unto him, Before the cock crow, thou shalt deny me thrice. And he went out, and wept bitterly. (Matthew 26:75)

Undoubtedly, Peter felt embarrassed by his failure. It is likely that he stood in doubt of his position before the Lord. However, when Jesus appeared to the disciples, he commanded Peter to go on and do what He had called for him to do.

He saith unto him the third time, Simon, son of Jonas, lovest thou me? Peter was grieved because he said unto him the third time, Lovest thou me? And he said unto him, Lord, thou knowest all things; thou knowest that I love thee. Jesus saith unto him, Feed my sheep. (John 21:17)

Though Peter failed, Jesus dined with him (a sign of friendship and fellowship) and charged him with ministry. This shows that after failure, if we go on with the Lord, we can receive from Him and expect to walk in the fulfillment of every promise made to us.

Jesus called the disciples from the beginning so that they would preach His word. If He condemned Peter, then His original plan for Peter would not have come to pass. He forgave Peter because He wanted Peter to walk in the purpose of God for his life.

Even after failure, the believer must continue to trust God's forgiveness and continue to develop relationship with Him. In doing so, every promise of God will manifest. When Jesus told the woman to go, it set her up for God to fulfill purpose in her life.

Walk in Righteousness

The woman, having received forgiveness, needed to do one more act. After instructing her to go, Jesus told her to sin no more. His statement has two implications. The first is that she was not to be caught in that same sin again. The second is that she was not to continue to live a life of sin. God offers forgiveness to believers so that they can overcome sin and not repeat sin.

> *And I gave her space to repent of her fornication; and she repented not. (Revelation 2:21)*

In the book of Revelation, Christ stated that He gave Jezebel, a space to repent. When God forgives, it provides space for the believer to overcome and not deliberately continue to walk in sin. Believers are not to continue to sin because God offers grace for forgiveness.

> *What shall we say then? Shall we*

continue in sin, that grace may abound? God forbid. (Romans 6:1-2a)

The woman taken in adultery had to have taken Jesus' words seriously. Her sins had put her in a life or death situation. Yet, she was able to survive it because of God's mercy. One king who demonstrates this in a more explicit manner was King Manasseh.

Manasseh was the son of Hezekiah. He knew God's law and saw the righteousness of his father. However, Manasseh was the complete opposite of his godly father.

Manasseh was twelve years old when he began to reign, and he reigned fifty and five years in Jerusalem: But did that which was evil in the sight of the Lord, like unto the abominations of the heathen, whom the Lord had cast out before the children of Israel. (II Chronicles 33:1-2)

Manasseh was a true 'bad boy.' Everything that was prohibited by God, he performed them. He committed idolatry, put idols in the house of the Lord, practiced witchcraft and sorcery, he operated in divination, he sacrificed his children to false gods, and the like.

The lives of some believers read like Manasseh's. They know God, but seem as if they cannot get it together.

Not only was Manasseh wicked, but also, he did not repent when the Lord spoke to him. Because of his wickedness, God allowed Manasseh to be dethroned, taken into captivity, and afflicted. Unlike other kings whom He slew, God spared his life, though he suffered.

> *Wherefore the Lord brought upon them the captains of the host of the king of Assyria, which took Manasseh among the thorns, and bound him with fetters, and carried him to Babylon. (II Chronicles 33:11)*

Manasseh's sins brought him into a life or death situation, like the woman. He lost his position as king and was jailed. Yet, Manasseh did something he had not done before. He humbled himself, repented, and prayed.

> *And when he was in affliction, he besought the Lord his God, and humbled himself greatly before the God of his fathers, And prayed unto him: and he was entreated of him, and heard his supplication, and brought him again to Jerusalem into his kingdom. Then Manasseh knew that the Lord he was God. (II Chronicles 33:12-13)*

Because of his humility, God heard Manasseh's prayer and restored him to his kingdom. *Again, if believers are sincere in their confession and repentance, God will restore them to their places in*

Him. This enables them to walk in expectation of His promises. Manasseh not only received God's forgiveness, but he walked in righteousness also. He did not return to his sin, but demonstrated his appreciation for God's forgiveness in his life.

Manasseh corrected his error and led Jerusalem and Judah in a spiritual renewal. He demonstrated Jesus' words of *sin no more.*

> *And he took away the strange gods, and the idol out of the house of the Lord, and all the altars that he had built in the mount of the house of the Lord, and in Jerusalem, and cast them out of the city. And he repaired*

the altar of the Lord, and sacrificed thereon peace offerings and thank offerings, and commanded Judah to serve the Lord God of Israel. Nevertheless, the people did sacrifice still in the high places, yet unto the Lord their God only. (II Chronicles 33:15-17)

Manasseh did not return to his many sins, but turned aside from them to righteousness. His story reveals that no matter how great our sin, God will forgive us if we come to Him in sincerity. In addition, Manasseh demonstrates that we can leave sin behind and walk in righteousness.

If Manasseh received forgiveness and

walked in God's favor, the believer who comes to God after sin and failure experiences the same. He has to remember to go and sin no more. If the believer will remember the words of Jesus to this woman, he or she will be able to leave out of their personal pits and enter into God's purpose for their lives.

Again, if Adam, Cain, Abraham, Jacob, the children of Israel, and many other notable figures received forgiveness to walk in God's favor, blessing, and promise, the believer today can do the same.

Previously, we discussed Israel. Israel's story, again, serves as the ultimate example. He brought them out of Egypt to enter into Canaan. He brings the believer out of sin and failure to enter into His promises.

The believer only has to remain persistent and consistent in his/her pursuit of God and His righteousness. The words of Paul should be a part of the daily prayer and meditation of believers.

> *Brethren, I count not myself to have apprehended: but this one thing I do, forgetting those things which are behind, and reaching forth unto those things which are before, I press toward the mark for the prize of the high calling of God in Christ Jesus. (Philippians 3:14)*

Though the believer falls, he has to get up again. God not only offers forgiveness, but strength for the journey. He gave Israel bread in the wilderness to sustain them until they reached Canaan. If the believer will receive God's help and strength through the Word of God, the presence of the Holy Spirit, and the encouragement of other Christians, he/she will come out of their personal pits and into the purpose of God.

If the believer walks in the words Christ spoke to the woman, he/she will overcome in the time of sin and receive strength in the time of failure. This will result in victory over personal defeat. More importantly, the believer will be able to forget the failures of the past and possess their God-given destiny.

Bibliography

Lockman Foundation. *Comparative Study Bible.* Zondervan Publishing House. Grand Rapids, MI, c1984

The Bible Library. *The Bible Library CD Rom Disc.* Ellis Enterprises Incorporated, (c) 1988 – 2000. 4205 McAuley Blvd., Suite 385, Oklahoma City, OK 73120. All Rights Reserved.

Merriam-Webster Online Dictionary. Copyright © 2005 by Merriam-Webster, Incorporated. All rights reserved.

www.ingramcontent.com/pod-product-compliance
Lightning Source LLC
Chambersburg PA
CBHW020512100426
42813CB00030B/3216/J